Contents

Go to the Beach

HOUGHTON MIFFLIN

BOSTON

Printed in China

ISBN-13: 978-0-618-93189-7
ISBN-10: 0-618-93189-9

1 2 3 4 5 6 7 8 9 SDP 15 14 13 12 11 10 09 08

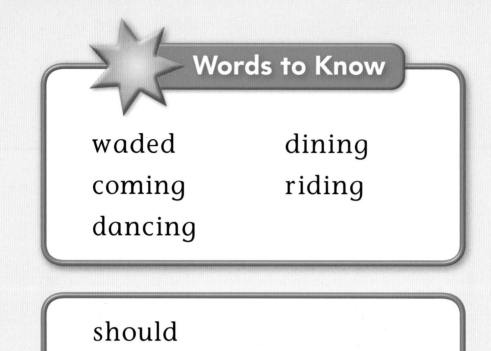

Words to Know

waded	dining
coming	riding
dancing	

should

Missing Sue

by Margaret Hall

illustrated by Karen Brooks

Amber has a neighbor named
Sue. Amber and Sue are best friends.
They like lots of the same things.

Amber and Sue like dancing in the dining room. They like riding bikes in the park. They like swimming in the town pool.

Right now Amber and Sue can't
play or dance. They can't ride bikes
or swim. Sue went to camp. She
will be at camp for six long weeks!
Amber misses her more every day.

Then a letter from Sue came in the mail. She wrote to Amber about Family Day at camp.

The letter said, "My mom and dad are coming to see me at camp. You should come with them if you can!"

Amber and Sue had lots of fun at camp. They waded and played in the waves. They danced on the sand and rode bikes near the beach. They had swimming races, too.

Amber is home again. She still
misses her best friend. Amber isn't
sad now, though. She knows Sue will
be home soon.

8

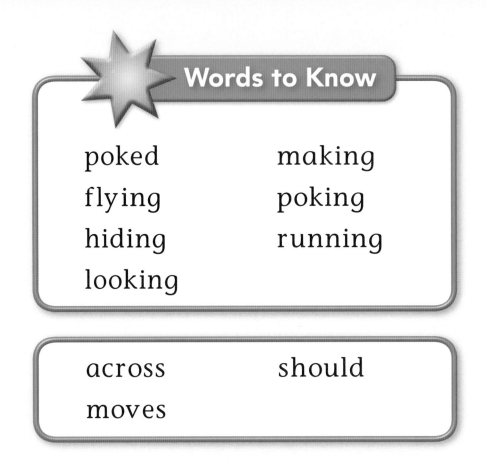

Words to Know

poked   making

flying   poking

hiding   running

looking

across   should

moves

Beach Animals

by Margaret Hall

Lots of animals are making their homes at this beach. These animals live in the water, under rocks, and in the sand.

Let's take a hike on the beach and see how many animals we can spot.

A stingray goes by in the water.
It has two wings and a long tail that
help it swim. When it swims, it
looks like it is flying under water.

This crab makes its home in an empty shell. The crab is hiding from seagulls. The shell should keep it safe if a seagull tries to eat it!

A fish is hiding, too. It just poked its nose out to see if it is safe. If a bigger fish gets close, this fish will stay hidden in the seaweed.

This starfish is in a tide pool. The starfish has five legs, but it moves quite slowly across the sand and rocks. It might find a rock and stick tightly onto it.

Seagulls are running on the sand. Their feet are making tracks in the wet sand. Soon the waves will take the tracks away.

Which of these animals would you like to see at the beach?